Here Is My Cat

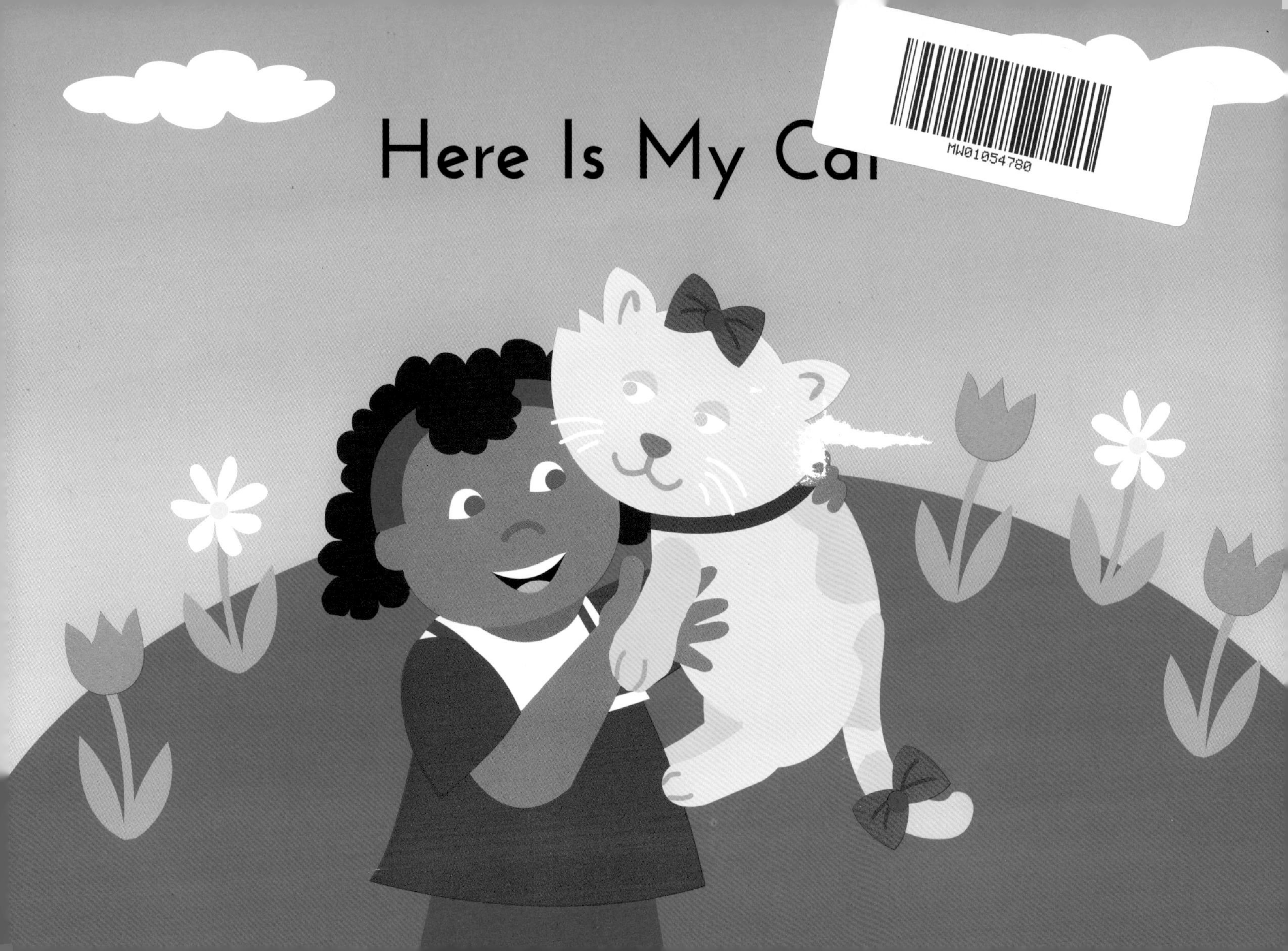

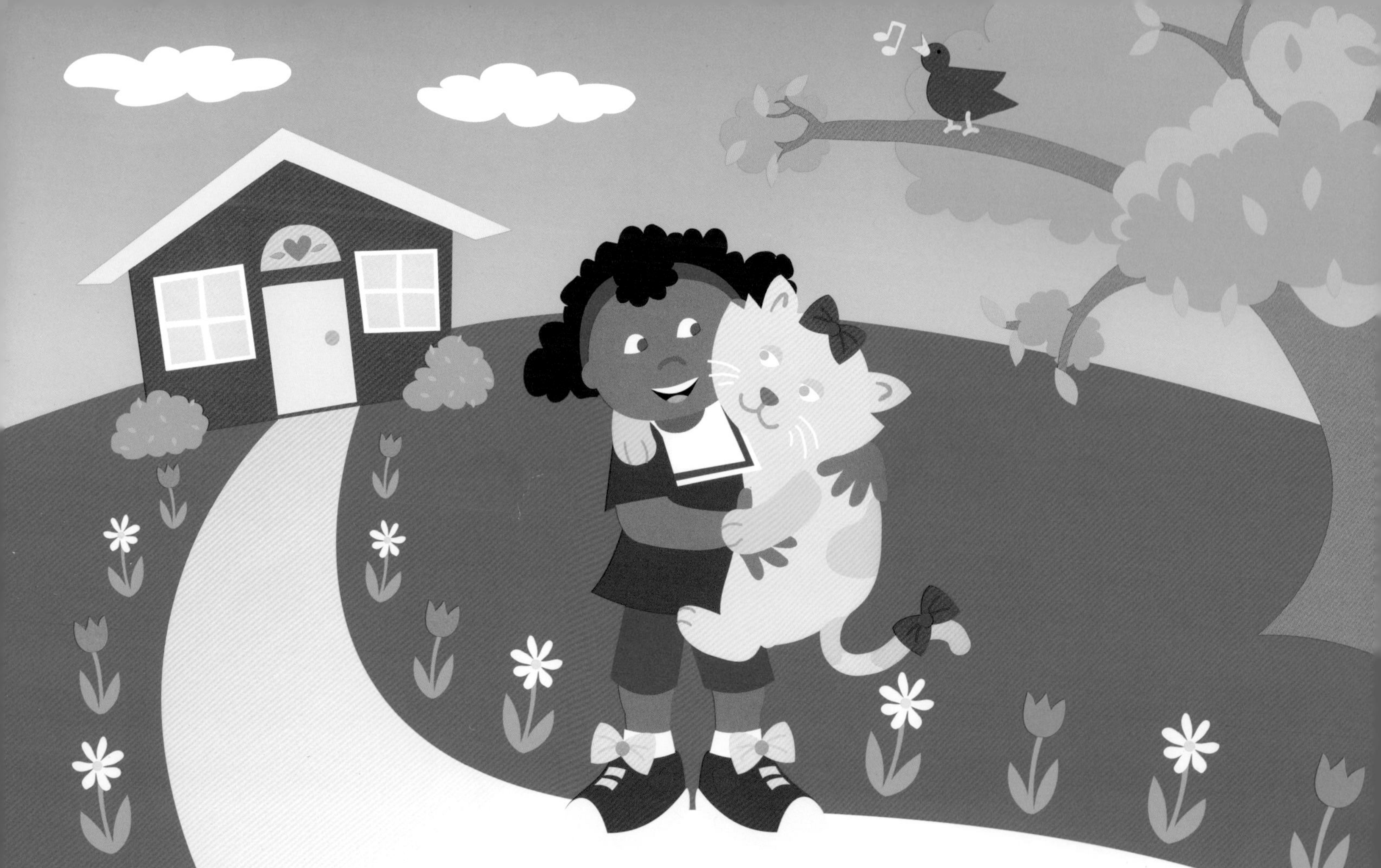

Here is my cat.

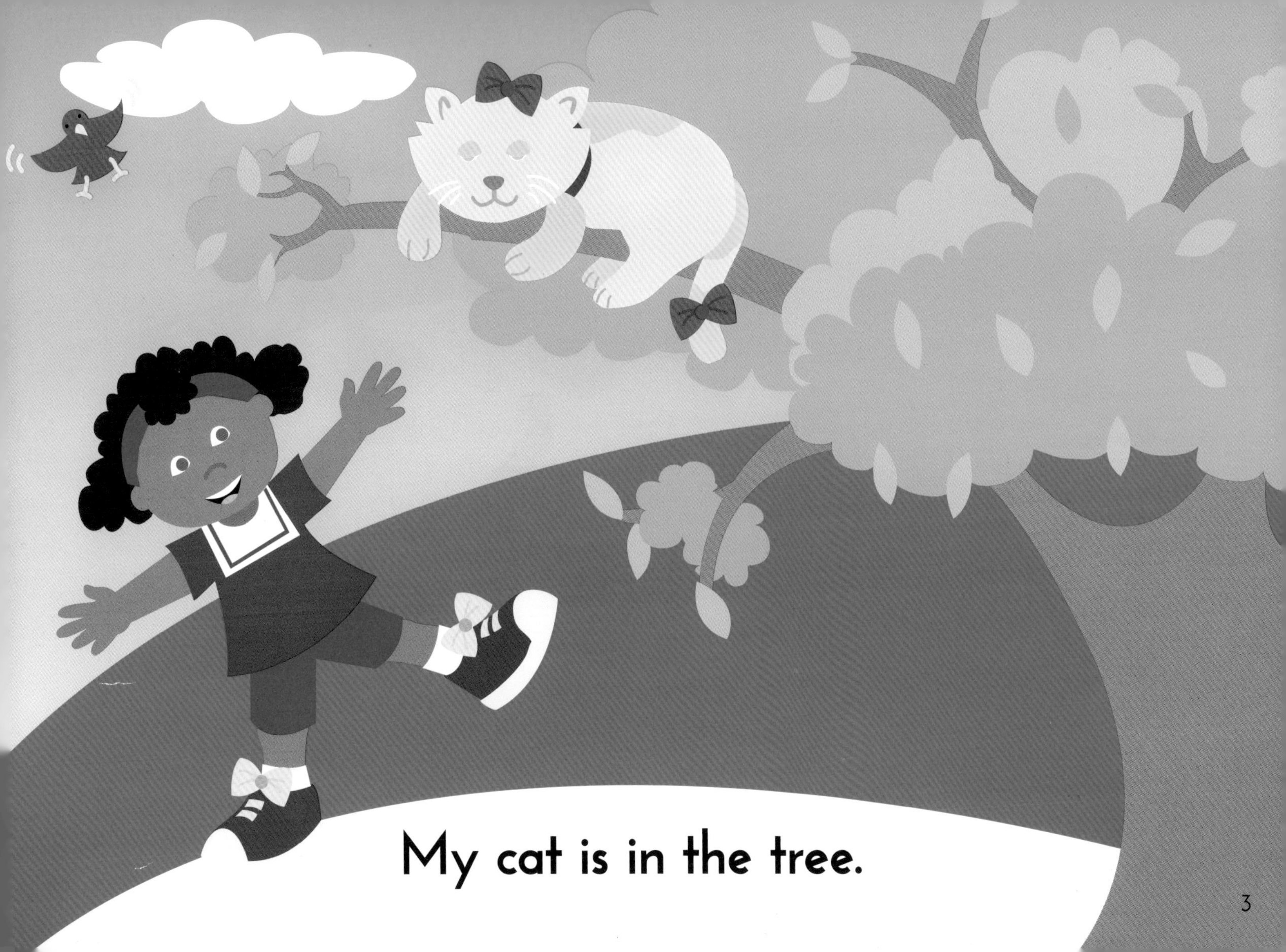

My cat is in the tree.

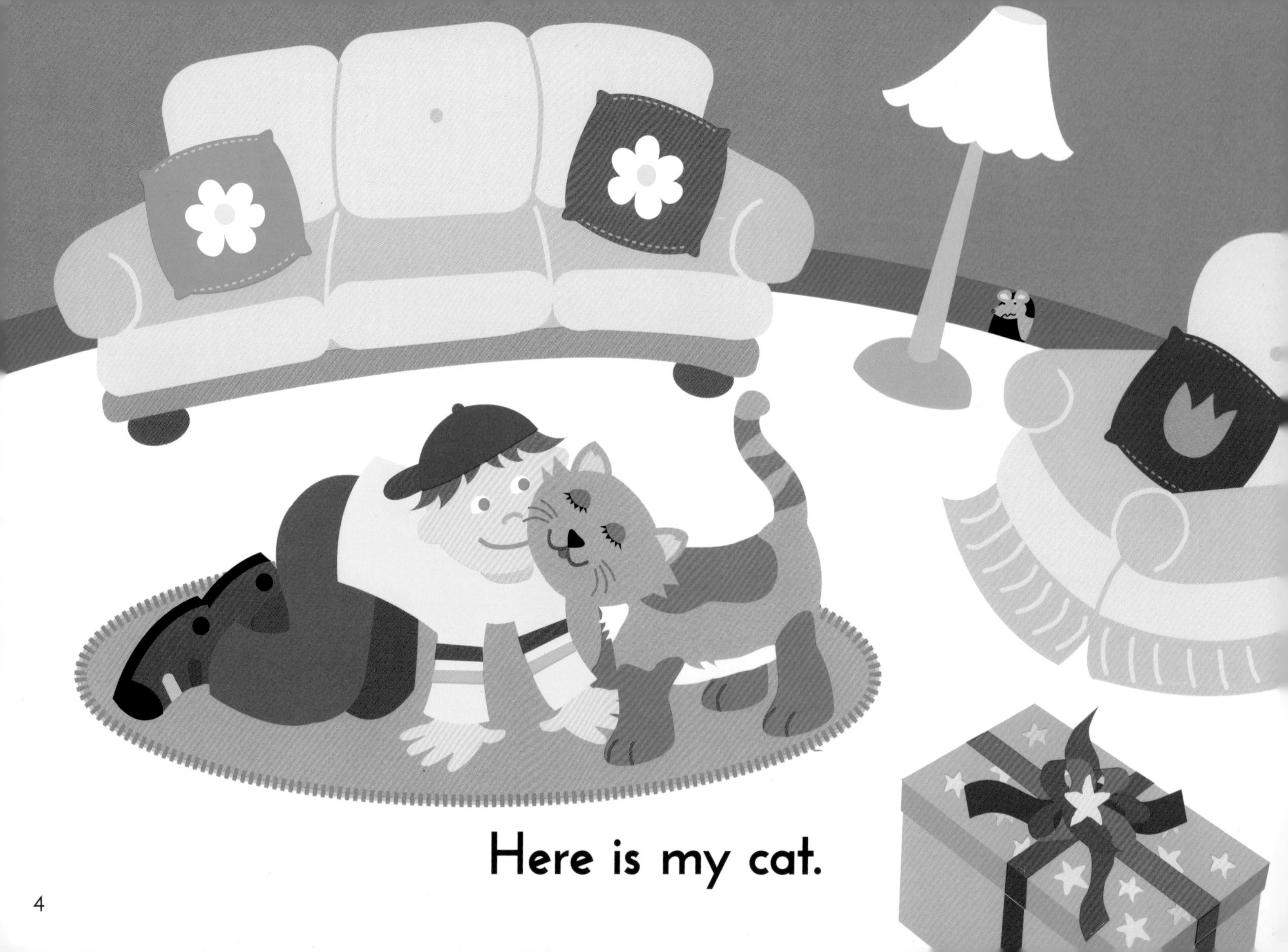

Here is my cat.

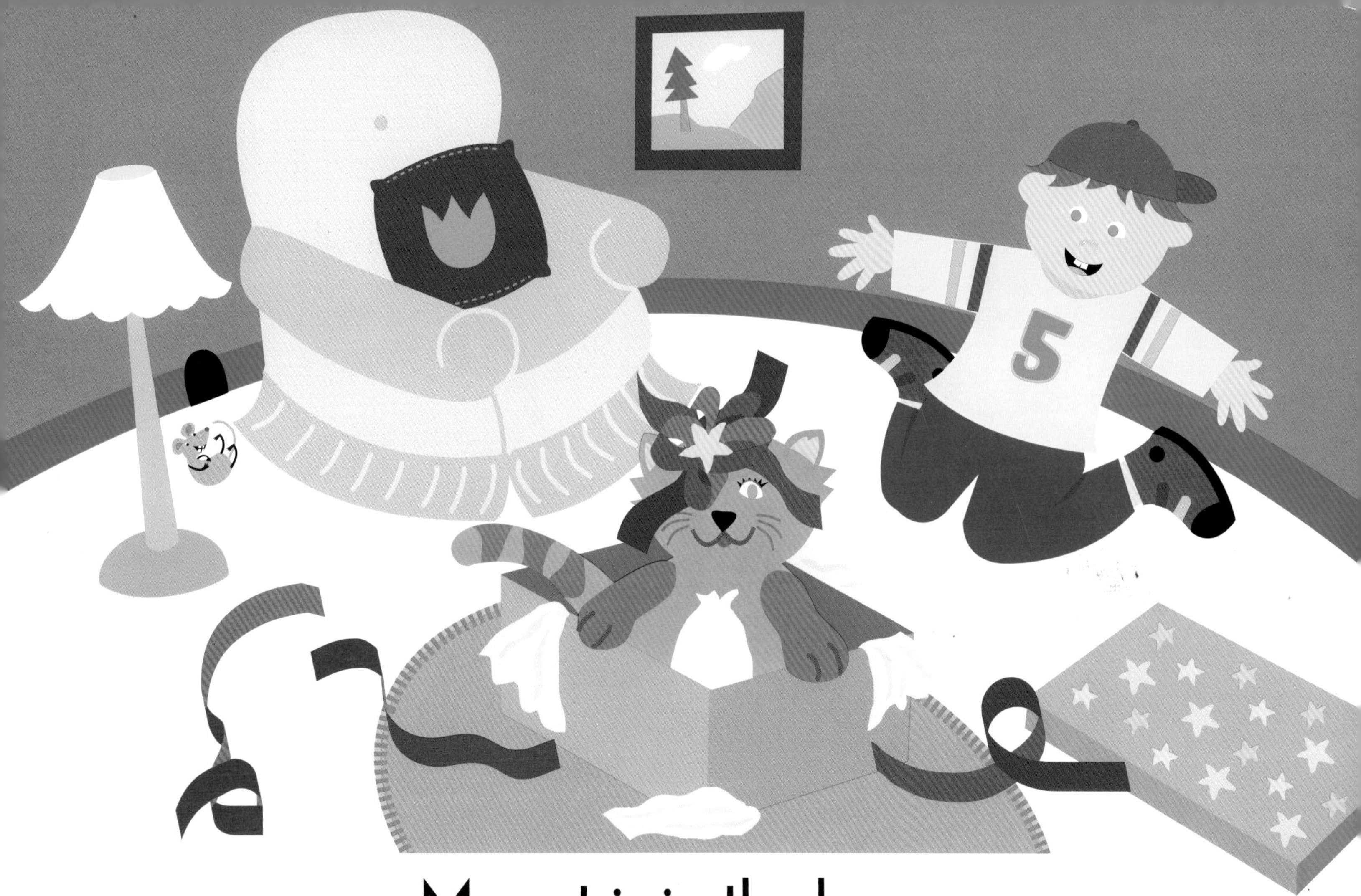

My cat is in the box.

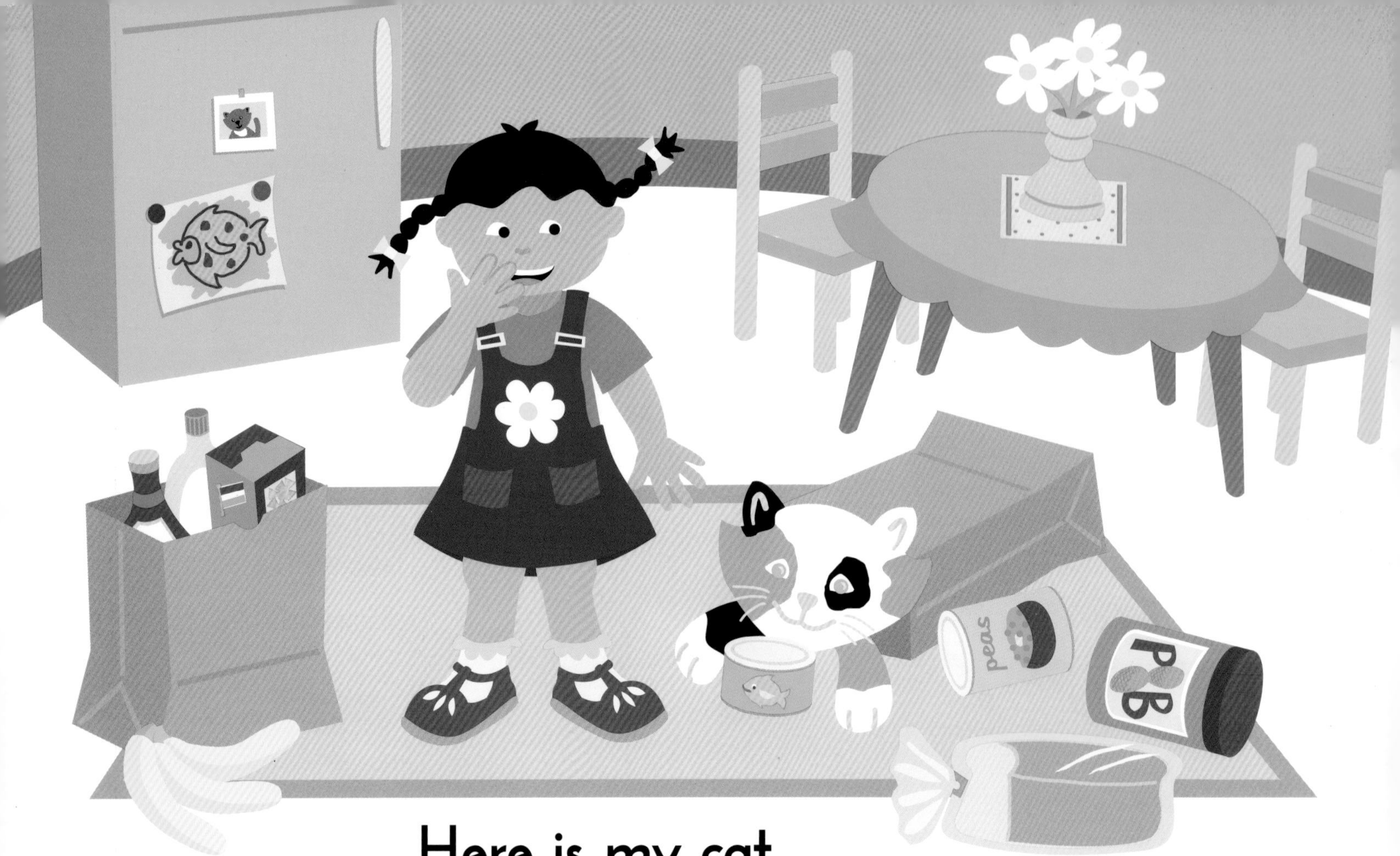

Here is my cat.
My cat is in the bag.

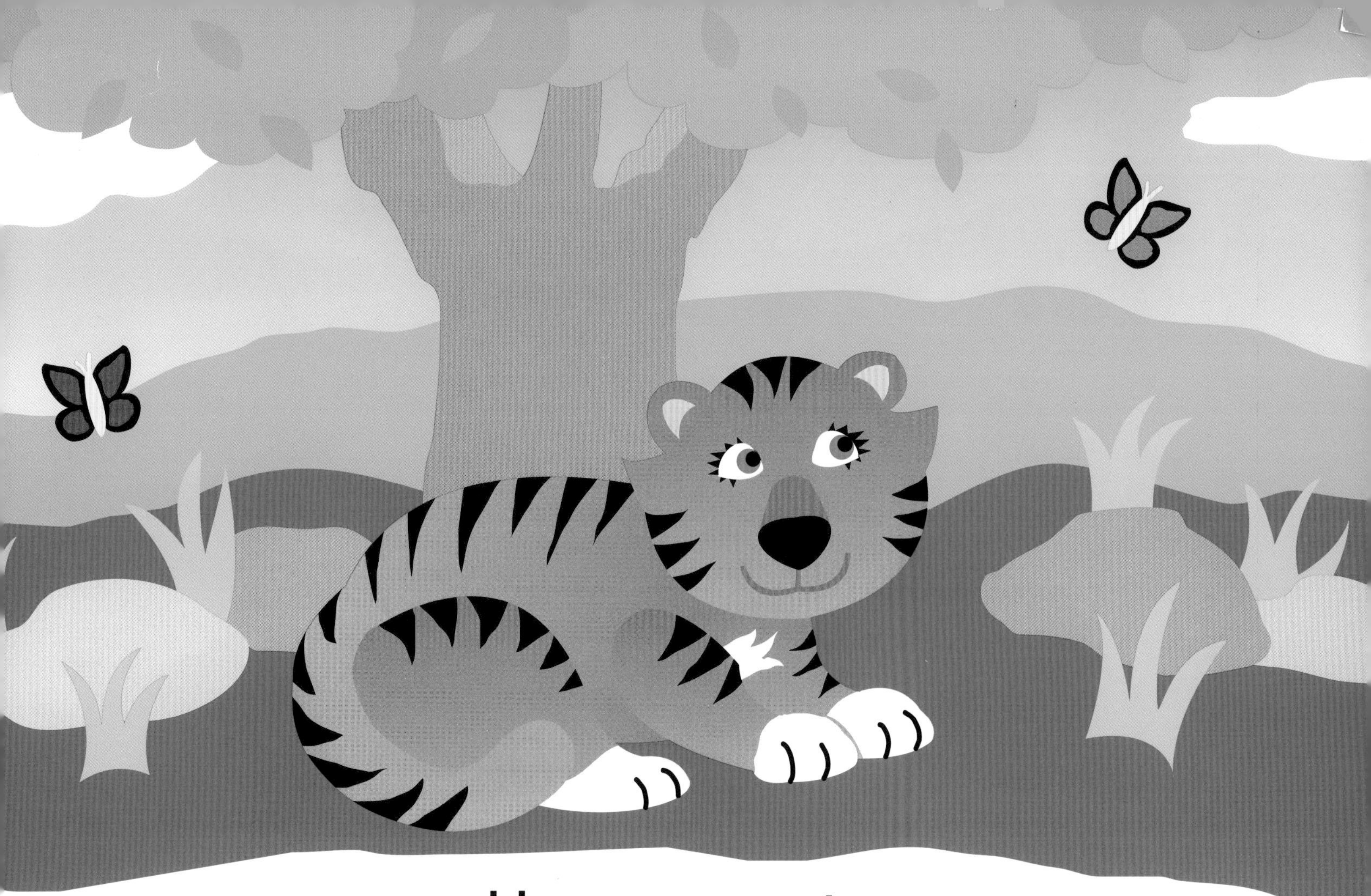

Here is my cat.

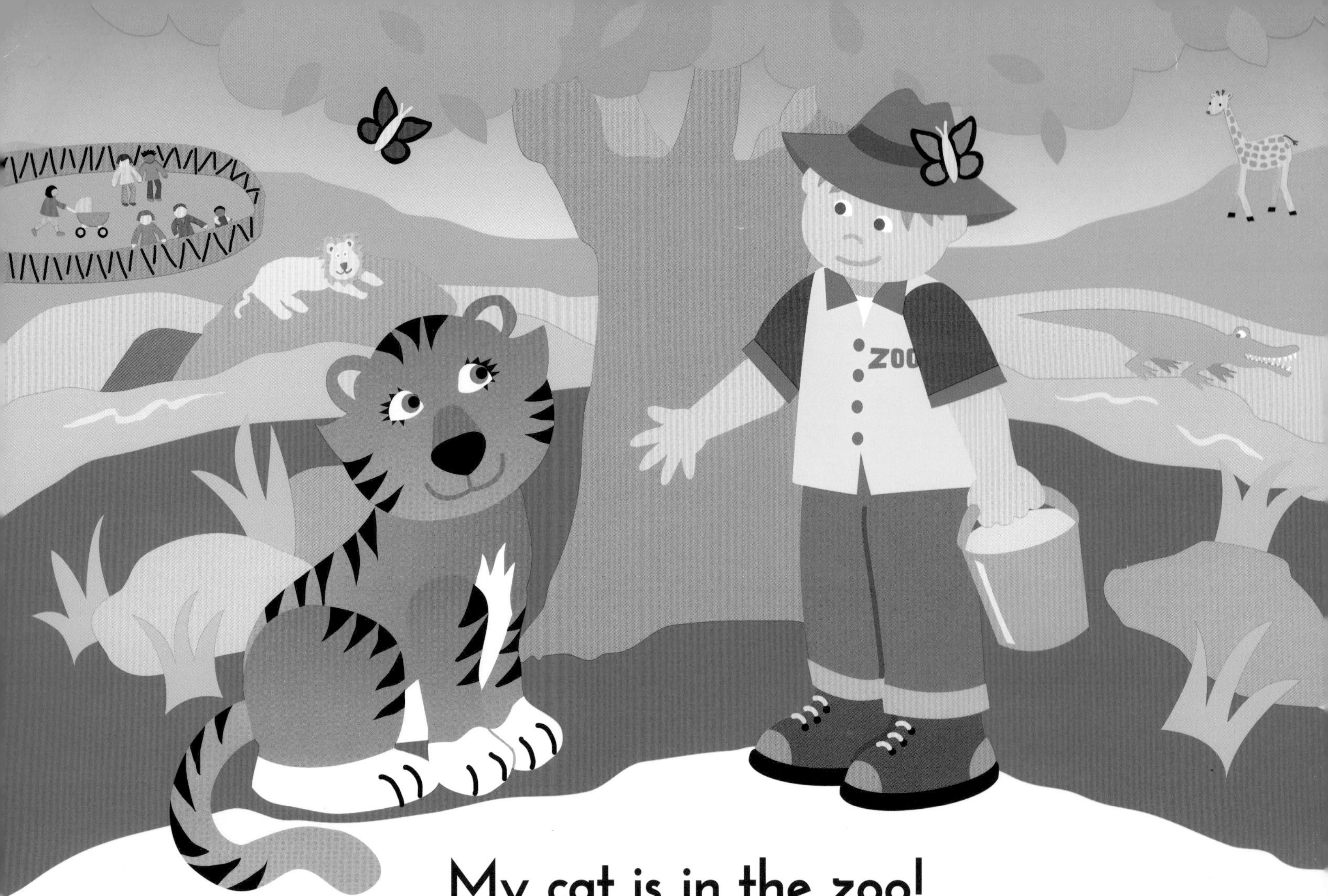

My cat is in the zoo!